EPITAPH FOR THE GIANTS

EPITAPH FOR THE GIANTS

The Story of The Tillamook Burn
by
J. Larry Kemp

The Touchstone Press
P.O. Box 401
Portland, Oregon 97207

Library of Congress Catalog Card Number 67-29848

first printing, September 1967

PHOTOGRAPHIC CREDIT
Joseph A. Bell, Sr.
William H. Grand
Forest Industries
Alfred A. Monner
Les T. Ordeman
Oregon Historical Society
The Oregonian
The Oregon Journal
Photo - Art Commercial Studios
U.S. Forest Service
Weyerhaeuser Company

PROLOGUE

In the one hundred and sixty years since Lewis and Clark wintered on the Pacific Coast, approximately two hundred billion board feet of timber have been killed by forest fires in Oregon alone, an average of one billion, two hundred million board feet a year.

The fires killed trees that were among the oldest living things on earth when the ancestors of the men who later inhabited Oregon Country landed at Plymouth Rock; huge trees that stood tall, straight as the masts of a square-rigged sailing vessel; thick, proud of their heritage of time, and beautiful in their color.

These friendly giants fed and warmed the Indians beneath their great, sheltering boughs, and the first white man to reside on Oregon's Tillamook Bay made his home in a hollow trunk, to him a castle.

As more families came to Oregon, the forest monarchs fell before the axe to make room for homes and farms. The trees provided the lumber for the farms, and timber for ships to bring more men. A cycle was thus created that contributed to the hellish ravage of the virgin forests, for with the men came the fires.

The first forest fires recorded in the Oregon coast range, which lies between the Willamette and Tualatin River Valleys and the Pacific Ocean, were caused by man. In 1845, a settler clearing land in the extreme western end of what is now Marion County started a fire that traveled west, rushed up the eastern side of the coast range and plunged down the western slopes to the sea, devastating the homes and hunting grounds of the Nestucca Indians. In 1878, hunters started a fire that roared south and west out of what is now Clatsop County into the present Tillamook County; again only the

sea stopped it. A man-set fire in 1902 claimed a portion of the Wilson River watershed in Tillamook and Washington Counties, and in 1918, a forest fire threatened the fine stands of spruce needed for aircraft production in World War I. A gyppo (contract) logger started a fire in 1931 that killed a forty-square mile area of giant trees on the Tillamook-Washington County line. Two million dollars in timber and property were lost in 1932 when what was then claimed to be the worst fire in logging history burned a swath through Tillamook County.

By comparison, these were minor incidents in the trials that the giants were to undergo.

More than two hundred fires of varying size and intensity burned in Oregon forests in the summer of 1933, but the general feeling of the public was that with so many trees, Oregon always would have fires and few paid much attention. Unless a fire was particularly spectacular or threatened a village, it seldom was noted in the local newspaper. Only logging operators cared when private stands of timber were threatened by a fire, and for them it was personal. In addition to the economic loss, the loggers had the hot, dangerous work of fighting the fire. Rangers of the state and national forest services cared, too, but their voices were not strong enough to be heard, yet.

In 1933, no improved roads penetrated the vast forest area between Portland and the northern Oregon coastal towns. A 1918 United States Forest Service map shows a military road, no more than a dirt track, winding from Forest Grove, twenty-three miles west of Portland, through Gales Creek, Elsie, and Jewell to Astoria and the coast. But, by 1933, underbrush had made the Elsie to Astoria portion of the road impassable. The balance mean-

dered from village to village with side tracks to logging camps along the way.

There was the old Trask Toll Road, also, that followed the Trask River from Tillamook back into the wilderness of Yamhill County. It had been established in 1871 as an outlet for settlers along the Trask, but by 1911 it was no longer used. The Wilson River Toll Road was constructed in 1893 as a mail and freight route for homesteaders living in the area from Gales Creek to Tillamook. Specifications called for it to be "eight feet in width the entire length with turnouts conveniently placed for wagons and teams to pass each other with safety." This road served the area until 1907 when violent disputes over tolls ended with its closure to all but an occasional rancher's wagon or stage.

Thus, the Southern Pacific Railroad was the only means of direct travel through the domain of the giants from Portland to Tillamook.

Today, several modern highways connect the deep-port city of Portland with the towns on the northern Oregon coast. Two of these, the Wilson River Highway, which since 1941 has followed the pioneer Wilson Toll Road route, and the Sunset (Wolfe Creek) Highway, opened in 1938, pass through areas of low-lying brush, stunted trees, and young saplings in the coastal range. The eye of a traveler on these routes is caught by a sight that resembles a ragged, broken comb, for silhouetted against the horizon of every rise are thousands of black, rotting snags. They stand stark, broken, and seared, surrounded by hundreds of windfalls, each a vivid reminder of a monster that devastated this once-lush paradise where the giants lived.

This inferno killed more than twelve billion board feet of prime timber in a raging twenty-hour period, a rate of more than six hundred million

A flatbed train, loaded with gigantic Douglas fir logs, heads out of the mountains in the early 1930's.

board feet an hour. It was the greatest single economic loss suffered by the State of Oregon, and was almost four times the property loss of the famous Chicago fire of 1871. Thousands of jobs went up in smoke, literally, at a time when Oregon, as all other states, was attempting a recovery from the great depression of 1929.

Miraculously, only one man lost his life.

Many of the largest timber companies in the Northwest suffered bankruptcy or near-bankruptcy because of the fire, and some of the world's finest fishing and hunting country was made a wasteland.

This is the story of that fire, the wildest, most devastating conflagration 20th Century America has seen. It is the story of The Tillamook Burn.

J.L.K.

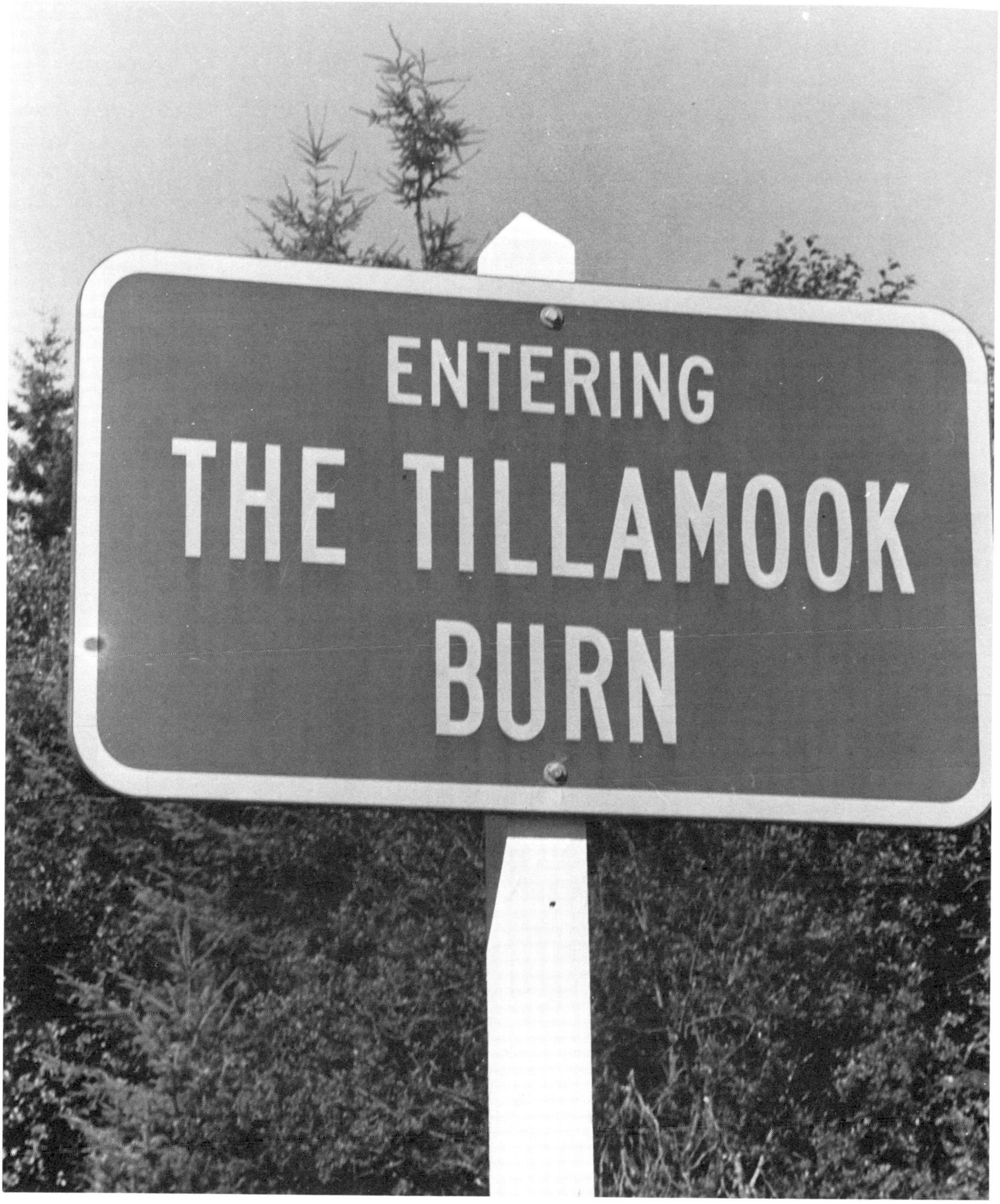
ENTERING
THE TILLAMOOK
BURN

AUGUST 14, 1933

It was already hot at dawn on Monday, August 14, heralding another scorcher in the sequence of broiling days in Oregon that summer. Portlanders suffered as the temperature soared above ninety degrees, an unusual level for this normally moderate climate. The fire danger was extreme in the state's forests, where the Douglas fir, hemlock, and pine had not felt a cooling rain for weeks.

After two months of exceptionally dry weather, Governor Julius Meier had ordered the state forests in southern and eastern Oregon closed, and he had pleaded with the loggers on the private lands in the northwestern counties to shut down.

When the humidity dropped to twenty-two percent in the foothills of the coast range, runners were sent from the main camps with orders for the local operations to shut down until fog, mist, or rain dampened the parched forest. At Glenwood, the one o'clock whistle sounded, and the crews had been back at their tasks about fifteen minutes when a messenger reached the gyppo operator working the slash and logged-over area of Gales Creek Canyon on the Crossett and Western Lands. The bullbuck was reluctant to shut down until he had loaded one more log that was being snaked out of the underbrush. His donkey engine huffed, and cables pulled taut, dragging a giant Douglas fir over a rotted windfall lying half-buried in the forest floor. As the two behemoths ground together, a spark jumped to the forest floor, where dry leaves and slashings of another logging era provided a fateful tinder, and the wind gave it life. "FIRE, FIRE," wailed through the glen.

Men in the camp grabbed axes, shovels, and picks and dashed to the fire area. They tried frantically to contain the flames, but were forced back

1

step by step as the wind fed the growing blaze. Men working farther away were called in but despite furious efforts, the fire ran over them.

At the South Saddle Mountain fire watch, ten miles southeast, a lookout saw the smoke. Hoffman lookout spotted it at almost the same moment. Simultaneously, they called their headquarters in Forest Grove. "Fire in Gales Creek Canyon!" In minutes, crews were on the way.

No fire roads allowed penetration of men and equipment into the forest, and no airplanes dropped smoke jumpers; these techniques had not been developed in 1933. This fight was a blood and sweat operation between muscular woodsmen with pick, axe, shovel, and dynamite and a fire that had everything going for it—wind, heat, humidity, dense underbrush, and the thick growth of the trees. All odds were in the ravager's favor.

The men in Gales Creek Canyon fought well through the afternoon and night, and by morning they were exhausted. But, the fire roared on unchecked toward virgin timber.

Floods in Kingston, Jamaica, and the new Boeing monoplane flights from Seattle to Portland made the headlines today in the Portland newspapers as did requests for shorter hours and higher pay asked for by the logger's union.

AUGUST 15, 1933

Tuesday was hotter still, with the temperature reaching one hundred and four degrees. At Gales Creek, weary men were ready to drop when fresh crews moved in to renew the fight with vigor. The woodsmen knew that if they could just have enough time to build fire trails and contain the fire on the

3

ground, they could conquer it. As the temperature went up, the humidity dropped still lower. The gusty east wind continued to drive the fire before it. Into the green timber it went, up into the branches and boughs the fingers of flame ran. The breeze grew stronger and the flames leaped higher.

"Look out! She's gonna' crown!" Fire had reached the tops of the tallest giants, where the wind whisked hot sparks, burning branches, and even blazing tree tops into the air. The wind carried flaming debris miles into unprotected virgin timber setting a series of new blazes. It was an unequal battle even for the fresh crews.

Late in the afternoon came word of a big spot fire, fifteen miles south, along the north side of the Wilson River. A burning tree top, carried by the wind from the Gales Creek fire, had invaded a completely new area. The Gales Creek fire had spawned a blazing offspring.

Now the men were fighting two fires and the Wilson River fire was fast becoming the bigger and more dangerous of the two, for it was burning in uncut forest areas.

The Wilson fire fighters had made a base camp at Rheer's place, a well-known fishing camp eighteen miles from Forest Grove, but that evening they evacuated the camp for fear they would be surrounded and cut off by the crowning fire. The wind sent the flames flying through the air and a second camp in a farmer's clearing had to be abandoned.

The South Saddle Mountain lookout reported the Gales Creek fire only a few miles from him now with flames bursting from tree tops and spreading in all directions. Down in the fire itself, sweating men with raw and bleeding hands, had to douse their tools in the creeks and rivers in order to cool them enough to touch. Every time the fire crowned they

A crowning fire, the most dreaded threat to fire-fighters.

5

were forced to retreat to keep from being surrounded by the inferno.

By evening, four hundred and fifty men were fighting the two fires, and while they seemed to be getting the north (Gales Creek) fire under control, the south blaze (Wilson River) was running wild through the green timber. Another hundred men were called in from the CCC camp at Bly in Southern Oregon, and additional loggers volunteered to try and smother the spot fires that had started in eleven different sections along the north side of the Wilson River road. Night fell and the glow of the fires lighted the sky for miles around; a hue that announced the funeral pyre for thousands of acres or prime timber and a portent of things to come..

On that stifling August day, the Southern Pacific Railroad ran an ad in *The Oregonian* featuring its Sun Break Special, an excursion from Portland through the coast range to the Tillamook beaches and return for $1.90. The historic frigate Constitution (Old Ironsides) was in the Portland headlines for it was tied up at Swan Island and open to visitors. Al Capone was making a bid for a new trial. Six inches of one column on the front page was devoted to the fires, in contrast to a full page ad, "Be Careful with Fire," on page five.

AUGUST 16, 1933

The Wilson River fire enlarged steadily throughout the morning. It crowned again and again, jumping two miles across the Wilson River road and starting seven more spot fires in green timber.

The Gales Creek fire was now under control; however, not before an eight-hundred-foot trestle on the Gales Creek logging line fell victim to the raging flames.

7

The temperature now dropped to the high eighties, and the humidity began to rise. Fire wardens saw some hope of containing the south fire if the wind conditions got better, although several spot fires had merged into a large, threatening mass of flames that stretched from Elliot Creek to the Devil's Lake fork of the Wilson River. The bridge over the Wilson River at the twenty-mile post was burned when flying debris set it aflame, cutting off road communications with Tillamook. Telephone connections between the Forest Grove headquarters and fighting crews were cut also when the fire burned portable lines.

Residents of Forest Grove felt the heat from the blistered forests and were warned that they might have to evacuate if the wind shifted suddenly. Portlanders and Willamette Valley residents were aware now of the conflagration raging through their forests, as great smoke clouds rolled into the sky by day and glowed a sullen red at night.

Newspapers had carried little about the fires up to now, but with the flames completely out of control, the fires captured space on the front page of every paper in the Willamette and Tualatin Valleys. Volunteers who flocked to Forest Grove to aid in the struggle were sent away because of a shortage of tools. No one had thought the fires would get so bad, and the equipment was just not available although the help was needed.

Along with the fire, yesterday's heat made news, as did rioting in Cuba, the pursuit of the Touhy Gang in Chicago, and the hourly wage conflict between loggers and employers. Loggers wanted forty-five cents an hour—the employers offered twenty-five cents.

AUGUST 17, 1933

The excessive heat of the last few days began to abate; the humidity was on the rise, and fog and mist were drifting in from the coast as the east wind died.

There were six hundred men on the south fire alone by today. Many were Civilian Conservation Corps (CCC) boys from Chicago and other midwestern cities, and from New York, New Jersey, and the Atlantic coast. These big-city boys went into the fire under the fretful eyes of the few experienced fire-fighters who supervised their activities. (When it was all over, several days later, the supervisors had much praise for these youth from the east who fought so long and hard to save the giants.)

The fire wardens saw a new opportunity to gain on the fires, as the fog, mist, and lack of wind gave them a chance to strengthen and widen the fire lines.

The Gales Creek fire was surrounded now with trails. But, its spawn, the Wilson River fire, was in an area where men could not be sent in because of the density of the forest growth and the ferocity with which the fire burned. Two crews were sent in this date; one to start a trail on the east side of the Wilson fire, and another to build a trail on the west; the crews would attempt to meet on the north side above the road. Trailing a fire is no simple operation under the best conditions, and trailing this one was a mammoth undertaking. The growth was like a rain forest; trees so thick they yielded as much as one hundred thousand board feet to the acre, more than enough timber to build sixteen five-room houses. The undergrowth was so heavy and dense it had to be chopped out with each step. The forest floor was covered with decayed vegetation six to twelve inches deep. Separate

9

gangs cleared away the underbrush before the men on the trail crews could begin digging through the forest floor to the soil and rock beneath. All through the day and well into the night the crews cut, slashed, dug, and blasted a huge swath through the brush and timber. Everything that would burn and allow the fire to continue its rampage was cut out. Trails up to fifty feet wide were denuded of any vegetation that could possibly feed the inferno.

The fire bosses knew they had a chance now. If the fog and mist held until the forest had a good dampening, the men could do the rest. At five o'clock a thick mist moved in along the western edge of the fires and hopes continued to rise. The bridge at the twenty-mile post was being repaired and the road was being cleared of fallen snags and debris. A sudden gust of wind forced one group of men to abandon a third camp at Zigzag on the Wilson River. They had to retreat over their own trail back to the camp evacuated previously at Rheer's place.

Late in the afternoon, portable telephone communications were reestablished between the men on the fire and Forest Grove headquarters.

The *Oregon Journal* carried three photos of the fire on the front page, and an editorial cartoon depicting forests under a cloud of smoke and dollars was labeled "carelessness."

Flooding in China, job increases, and a new suspect in the Lindbergh kidnapping also made news in today's newspapers.

AUGUST 18, 1933

By Friday more than one thousand men were on the fire lines. Everyone was needed. The mist evaporated, and the fog blew away as the east wind started to rise again. The crews did everything

10

they could to hold the fire on the ground, but the freakish breeze took it straight up into the tree-tops, where it crowned wildly, moving west with the speed and roar of an express train. It jumped the fire lines like a school girl playing hopscotch, and rushed on to new conquests in the fresh timber while the men ran for their lives.

The Wilson spawn had exceeded the sire in size and fierceness.

For two days this outbreak would run rampant while men and equipment poured into the little headquarters at Forest Grove. CCC tree rangers from Molalla were trucked to the fire camp. They were equipped, but what they did not have, the U.S. Army brought from Vancouver barracks and soldiers set up facilities to feed and house the firefighters. This small city of eighteen hundred persons suddenly looked like an embarkation center for an all-out war. Army officers volunteered to command some of the contingents in the woods and to take care of the logistical support involved in order to leave the fire wardens to concentrate on the strategy of fighting the fire. Trucks rolled on a twenty-four hour basis from Portland and the Willamette Valley cities. Washingtonians from Vancouver helped with equipment, supplies, and men. Trucks rumbled out of Forest Grove to the miles of new fire lines that were being established in the hope the wind would soon cease to play its deadly game.

The fire now covered more than twenty-five square miles of dense forest, and papers talked about it in every edition. They talked also about the state liquor tax, an avalanche on South Sister Mountain in central Oregon, and a nude wild man hiding out in the woods around Tillamook Head.

AUGUST 19, 1933

This was a day and night of a valiant clash of man against nature, but no human force could stand before the masses of flame that roared out of the conflagration, seemingly burning nothing, across the denuded firebreak to clutch at the green timber on the other side.

More than twelve hundred men were known to be fighting the south fire now, and many others were not even counted. Farmers and ranchers were toiling to save their homes and livestock; loggers to save their future jobs. In Gales Creek Canyon, three hundred fifty men were trying to save anything they could. By evening it looked as if the battle-weary men might again have a chance. The humidity was up, making the atmosphere sticky. The east wind had suddenly ceased to play fast and loose with the flames. Fire lines were holding as the blaze grounded. Although burning furiously within, the fire had stopped traveling like a satanic tornado. It appeared to be checked.

The fire bosses were cautious, for this had happened before. They continued to build lines and trails around the clock. But, things looked better and some of the urgency left their efforts.

Sunday, they thought, would be a fairly good day, at least by the standards of the past few days. The night crews of fresh men came on and the day gang retired to camp for a well-deserved rest.

All was better—an evening in camp without fear of being burned out, hot chow, a bed in which to sleep. Many of the men were veterans of action in the trenches in France a few years before, where they had faced enemy charges, artillery barrages, and German machine guns. They said they would rather do it all over again than face a fire such as this. The people of Forest Grove did their

Feeding the firefighters.

13

utmost for the tired, smoke-blackened men, as Saturday eased into Sunday.

Miraculously, the men had held the two fires to a combined area of approximately twenty thousand acres, in spite of the quirks of the wind. This was bad enough, but not nearly what it might have been had the fire got any more help from the winds and humidity.

By evening the fire had dropped from sight as far as the papers were concerned. There was coverage of the Berbers' war with the French, the proposed Bonneville Dam project on the Columbia River, a new minimum wage of forty-two cents an hour for loggers, and the beer tax being the third largest money-maker for Uncle Sam.

AUGUST 20, 1933

Sunday morning was spent much as the night before had been. On the Wilson fire, the "on" crews worked at enlarging the fire lines, while those off duty relaxed or cleaned and repaired equipment. The fire bosses hoped the worst was over, but kept an eye open for tell-tale signs of weather changes and a recurrence of the fire. This monster needed watching for, like a sleeping dragon, it was only resting before unleashing its fury once again.

Suddenly, like a gigantic yo-yo, the east wind rose again, blowing with renewed vigor. The grounded fire leaped to this new prod with terrifying force, moving so rapidly that it caught the wardens completely by surprise. It flashed toward two CCC camps, burning out both in a matter of minutes, then moved on to demolish a logging operator's headquarters. Nothing was saved by the frantic inhabitants as they retreated. The fiendish winds developed a circle of fire that moved in

on the rim of one camp from all directions, forcing hard-pressed crews to flee through the flames. To stand and fight was to invite incineration.

The same wind, rising to great force, swooped down on the semi-dormant Gales Creek fire, driving it to the fringes of green trees again, then sending it slicing through the forest like a scythe through a stand of ripe wheat.

Fortunately no one had been killed, but exhausted, beaten men began to drift into Forest Grove and Tillamook. Fire fighters with scorched, raw hides, heat prostration, and just plain fatigue staggered into first-aid stations where they were treated for singed hair and eyebrows, blistered and bleeding hands. One man had been crushed against a stump by a sliding truck, but he lived. Others suffered twisted knees, ankles, wrists, and backs from falls occurring as they attempted to negotiate the rough terrain in the fire area.

The fire apparently was counted out by the newspapers. They had it all over but the mopping up. The fact that "Old Ironsides" used Oregon Douglas fir for her masts and spars was played up big on the front pages in Portland.

The violence in Cuba continued to be news.

AUGUST 21, 1933

Erratic winds, that seemed to blow in all directions, carried the fire to the south and north while keeping steady pressure on the blazes moving west toward Tillamook and the coast. Residents of Forest Grove stood sickened as they realized the hope of a promised industrial boom for their city was ablaze in the nearby hills. The Stimson Lumber Company's holdings, which until now had been thought comparatively safe, were mowed down by the monster this morning. The new Stimson Mill, under

17

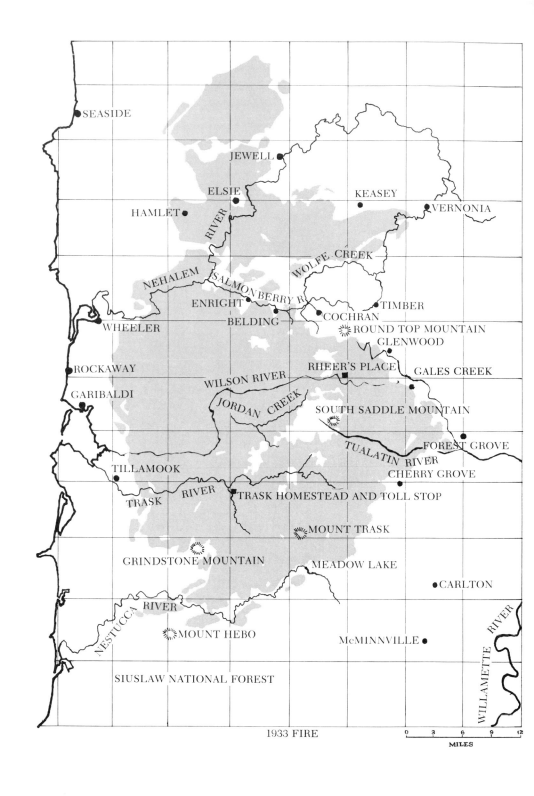

SEASIDE

JEWELL

ELSIE

KEASEY

HAMLET

VERNONIA

RIVER

WOLFE CREEK

NEHALEM

SALMONBERRY R.

ENRIGHT

TIMBER

BELDING

COCHRAN

ROUND TOP MOUNTAIN

WHEELER

GLENWOOD

ROCKAWAY

RHEER'S PLACE

GALES CREEK

WILSON RIVER

GARIBALDI

JORDAN CREEK

SOUTH SADDLE MOUNTAIN

TUALATIN RIVER

FOREST GROVE

TILLAMOOK

CHERRY GROVE

TRASK

RIVER

TRASK HOMESTEAD AND TOLL STOP

MOUNT TRASK

GRINDSTONE MOUNTAIN

MEADOW LAKE

CARLTON

NESTUCCA RIVER

WILLAMETTE RIVER

MOUNT HEBO

McMINNVILLE

SIUSLAW NATIONAL FOREST

1933 FIRE

0   3   6   9   12
MILES

construction in Scoggins Valley just south of Forest Grove, was in danger of the same fate. The headwaters of the Tualatin River were in the fire now and the flames were sweeping down the upper slopes of Scoggins Valley. Workmen at the mill site were pressed into service to fight this new threat.

People in Forest Grove could feel the heat of the fire, and the city fire department worked with unending effort to cover all the grass, brush, and house fires started by flying sparks and firebrands.

Women and children were kept busy in Forest Grove and other towns in the fire area smothering hot coals and burning leaves that fell from the red haze that hovered over everything.

Tremendous clouds of smoke boiled up over the mountains as more and more spot fires started in formerly untouched areas. The smoke added considerable confusion to the reports coming into headquarters from the various lookouts as they tried to keep track of each new blaze.

By now the south fire had jumped the Wilson River and was burning uncontrolled on both banks. Men sent to this site reported that it would mean suicide to attempt to get through the thick underbrush to try and surround the fire. All they could do was fight where they stood and hope and pray for the wind to die or, for a much-needed rain to soak the area.

The inferno seemed bent on vengeance as well as destruction. Tom Stevens, the lookout who had first reported the smoke in Gales Creek, called headquarters to say that the fire was moving toward South Saddle Mountain at tremendous speed. He figured he had one-half hour to get out and he was leaving his post. Minutes later the fire was raging up the side of the mountain toward the lookout, and soon it was curling around the cabin and

19

the base of the one-hundred-foot crows nest while little fingers of flame searched through the undergrowth for a vanished prey.

The Wilson River Road was again clogged with fallen trees and burning brands, and passage was restricted to one truck at a time, and then very slowly. Headquarters resembled a railroad dispatcher's office with drivers calling from various spots on the road to check for clearance to pass to the next telephone stop.

That evening the papers made much of ex-president Hoover being called as a witness in the Senate investigation on banking, and the National Recovery Administration was preparing to swing into action locally. The fire was back on page one, along with announcement that child labor was to end August 31, and notice of the fourth birthday of Princess Margaret of England. The biggest headlines were allocated to the State of Missouri which had voted to repeal prohibition.

AUGUST 22, 1933

The mercury climbed back into the nineties and the humidity dropped to twenty-one percent. The flames had almost reached the crest of the range in some areas, and residents of the coastal towns could see bright-orange fire tongues licking distant mountain tops. Reports in Tillamook stated that the fire was advancing on the city of "Trees, Cheese and Ocean Breeze" on a fifteen-mile front.

New menaces appeared. Fire caused by faulty machinery broke out at the Cadwalader and Davis Mill at the headwaters of the Yamhill River in the Trask Mountains, and quickly spread into slash and uncut timber surrounding it. The mill was leveled and the crew forced to flee. Oddly, a log-

Crews inspect the bridge across Devil's Lake Fork of the Wilson River, which burned early in the fire.

21

Headwaters of the Wilson
River before the 1933 fire

Headwaters of the Wilson
River after the 1933 fire.

ging truck left blazing at the site was found later almost completely destroyed except for the gasoline tank that was nearly full.

A careless camper had left a smoldering campfire near Jordan Creek (a tributary of the Wilson River), and soon a new fire raced into the timber, out of control almost as soon as it started.

The Wilson River fire, propelled by the wind, rushed toward the mountain tops and leaped the road again further south. Flying debris started another spot fire even further south on the headwaters of the Trask River; Mount Hebo and Trask lookouts both reported smoke so thick that they could not pinpoint the location immediately.

The Pacific Telephone and Telegraph Company reported a threat to their long distance telephone connections with Tillamook, as another spot fire burned near their building in the Trask Mountains. The Southern Pacific Railroad ceased running its Sun Break Special and all other passenger traffic through the burn as railroad crews were needed to protect their right-of-way. A crew with an engine and a tank car patrolled day and night, from Tillamook through Timber and Cochran, soaking down tunnels, trestles, and ties, and putting out spot fires near the tracks. Down in the fire it was so hot that trucks running supplies to men on the fire lines returned to headquarters with the paint on the cabs and fenders blistered or melted off, as if they had been in a gigantic oven. Wooden truck beds were charred and smoldering. Drivers feared for their lives as trees along the side of the road exploded with a roar, hurling chunks of burning wood as big as a man at the trucks.

Weather conditions continued to worsen as the day wore on. Just before dusk, heavy smoke was seen in the area of the State Fish Hatchery, ten

The burned trestle and twisted tracks at Gale's Creek.

25

miles east of the main Wilson River fire, indicating a new spot fire there. The main fires now covered a spotty front fifteen to eighteen miles wide and were burning with intense heat to a depth of five to seven miles. Until now the monster had followed the cuts and canyons in its climb to the mountain tops. Suddenly it looked as though it was joining forces all along the line for a concentrated rush over the crests, down the slopes, and to the sea. Fire wardens expressed concern also that the fire might blow up.

This morning Portlanders read about the Wilson River fire and a five-column picture showed the drama. Oregon's logging payroll was up to twelve million dollars, and Rudy Vallee and Alice Faye had been involved in an auto accident. Norfolk, Va., had just had six and one-half inches of rain.

AUGUST 23, 1933

The coastal towns of Tillamook, Wheeler, Garibaldi, and many other villages were under a pall of smoke. Doctors reported a tonsillitis epidemic brought on by the breathing of too much smoke. Ashes lay like dust on the streets and buildings and housewives complained that it was impossible to keep a house free of the gray-black plague that penetrated even closed windows and doors.

Eighteen hundred to two thousand men were moving into the fire from Tillamook. They would attempt to work their way north and south around the main blaze and join forces with the men fighting deep within the fire itself in hopes that sheer numbers would prevail where all else had failed.

As suddenly as the wind had come up, it died. Fog from the coast rolled over the fire zone and

CCC crews, who moved into the fire from Mt. Hood National Forest, won the praise of veteran forestry officials.

27

again the wardens tried to take advantage of this new opportunity. One hundred and seventy-five more men from Waldport and Forest Grove were sent to build and blast new fire trails. The Floras Logging Company sent seventy-five more men to battle the Yamhill blaze, which was on its land, and by afternoon they seemed to have it under control. The camper's fire on Jordan Creek was reported burning itself out. The only real danger now seemed to be the big spot fire in the Trask watershed and the Wilson River fire. These were still burning wildly but with the mist and fog moving in again, the temperature down to fifty-two degrees, and the humidity on the rise, the wardens saw a chance of bringing these red devils to heel.

Another blaze had popped up in an old burn along the Salmonberry River but wardens at the scene reported it under control, with more men available if needed to contain it.

The area now covered by the fires was forty-thousand acres from the headwaters of the Yamhill and Trask in the south, through the Wilson River, north to the Salmonberry River. Spot fires still moved slowly down the Trask toward Tillamook, but wardens in the area were confident of controlling them if the fog and mist held and the wind cooperated.

This slight calm gave the men a chance to check their equipment. Many tools had been lost or broken; many more had been cached in streams to save them from the flames when the defenders were forced to flee before the crowning fires. Mule teams were dispatched to controlled fire areas to bring back hundreds of abandoned tools.

Seventy percent of the portable telephone lines and instruments used on the fire lines had been destroyed. Instruments had been left behind when

29

the flames moved so rapidly that the men were compelled to drop everything and save themselves. An appeal to the Pacific Telephone and Telegraph Company brought an immediate response; instruments, miles of wire, and men to string it would be on the way tomorrow, although the company was still concerned for the safety of its long-distance lines between Tillamook and Forest Grove. Spot fires still burned only a mile or two from the long-distance lines, and the company's men were needed to protect them.

The finding of Mexican Emperor Maximilian's crown jewels and the forty billion bushel wheat surplus made news this morning, along with a one-column story about the fire. More government action on the Bonneville Dam project seemed apparent for the very near future.

AUGUST 24, 1933

Just before dawn the humidity plummeted to its lowest reading of the fire. The east wind began to gust again and then blow with ever-increasing steadiness, hurling the fire into the unburned timber. Fire wardens, with a sixth sense for danger, sent messengers to order all the fire crews, farmers, ranchers and their families on the south and west sides of the main fires to evacuate immediately. Cars were sent to help get them out. The orders were not to try and take anything, just get out— quickly! The dirt roads were choked with men, women, and children in the exodus. By afternoon the ethos of disaster was stronger.

Then it happened. The fire blew up! It blew forty thousand feet straight up! A great orange wall of flame eighteen miles across the front of

the fire exploded out of the treetops. All the fires became one enormous inferno, belching smoke and flame up, up, up into the heavens. A cloud forty miles wide mushroomed into the sky, to hang dull red, angry, and ominously over the blaze. As the winds above the cloud gained momentum, superheated air rushed upward like a geyser, carrying burning brands, hot coals and ashes with it. The flaming mass was carried far out over the ocean; ships five hundred miles at sea were pelted with smoldering rubbish raining from the sky. The sea rejected these charred fragments and for thirty miles along the coast the beaches were littered with debris, in some places to a depth of two feet.

The fire created its own hurricane. The hot air rushing up was replaced by fresh air, bringing more oxygen to the flames. The wind created by the inversion was frightening, its roar fantastic, its force incredible. It swooped on the burning trees plucking out fir two hundred and fifty feet tall as though they were seedlings, swirling them through the air, throwing them back to the conflagration.

Now the fire took its first and only life. Frank Palmer, a CCC tree ranger from Marseilles, Illinois did not meet a fiery death, but he was crushed by a great living tree uprooted by the hurricane and thrown at him as though the elements were playing some sort of horrible practical joke.

The fire headquarters was in total confusion. All portable telephone lines into the fire were out, but the smoke was so thick lookouts could not have reported with any degree of accuracy. Reports came in by word of mouth. Some were true, some distorted, and others completely false. The town of Cochran was reported completely destroyed, again. Elsie and Timber reportedly were surrounded and would soon suffer the same fate. Wheeler, on

Smoke clouds raced 40,-00 feet over The Burn, and debris rained on ships 500 miles at sea when the fire blew up.

33

the coast, was in extreme danger; residents were burying their valuables and preparing to leave. Long-distance telephone lines were out. The Telephone Company reported that it had lost contact with Tillamook. Nothing was known of the men who had been trying to save the telephone equipment and cabin up in the Trask Mountains. Tillamook was said to be in serious danger for it had been reported that the fire had rushed down the slopes of the mountains at terrific speed, to within four miles of the city. There were tales of wild train rides out of the mountains; of women and children clinging precariously to charred flat cars as trains rushed over smoldering trestles, charged around curves at dizzying speeds with walls of flame on either side; of throttles so hot engineers could not touch them, yet could not let go.

The bridge at the twenty-mile point on the Wilson River was reported burned again and so was the Red bridge, fifteen miles up river from Tillamook. No trucks could get through from those points into the Trask or Wilson areas now. The old Trask Toll House and stage stop was gone and the Rheer's place was burned partially. The fate of the people there was unknown. There was no way of separating fact from fiction.

Telephone Company crews went onto the fires with their wire and portable equipment despite the danger, and communications with Forest Grove were established slowly. Four more long-distance lines were being strung down through Corvallis, over to Newport and up the coast to Tillamook. Soon all communications would be in operation.

In Tillamook, and other coastal towns, the sun was blotted out completely by the cloud of smoke, and noon seemed to be midnight. Old timers called it the darkest day in history, Black Thursday.

Dwarfed by the giant trees, a lineman searches for the remnants of long distance telephone lines in the Trask Mountains.

35

Throughout the day little shafts of light filtered through the clouds in constantly changing hues. Weird colors of amber, yellow, and red would suddenly change to orange and a sickly blue depending on the thickness of the cloud bank. Newspaper photographers were forced to use flash bulbs during hours that normally are lighted by the sun. Mothers, not believing the reports of the fire's distance from Tillamook, kept their children home all this day and the next. Ashes and fir needles, moss and leaves filtered down through the overcast to cover Tillamook and nearby towns with litter. Gardeners complained as the droppings covered the flowers. White clothing was blackened. Some people were awakened by what they thought was blessed rain, but found instead unburned fir needles that had been swept up by the terrific drafts, carried west by the gale, and lowered through the quiet air on the coastal region to play a soft tattoo on the rooftops. At mid-day chickens went to roost and birds were quiet in the trees. Cows came home from the pasture and nuzzled barn doors seeking admittance. Dogs howled mournfully. Cars, when they moved, moved only with their lights on. Visibility was only a few hundred feet. All traffic moving to the burn area was supervised closely to keep out sightseers who would only impede traffic on the already congested road.

Despite the lack of communications the battle went on, each crew fighting independently.

More men were rushed to the fire lines. Volunteers came from all over Oregon. Men from Seaside, Astoria, and other coastal towns moved in from the west; from the east came recruits from Portland and Mt. Hood National Forest, more CCC youth, and loggers from the pine forests of eastern

Oregon.

But the fire raged on relentlessly, crazily. It leaped over the canyons, crags, and gullies, killing thousands of the giants as it went. It swept over the crests of the coast range and down toward the sea like a juggernaught undaunted by the puny efforts of thousands of mere humans trying to tame it. The heat was so intense that it cracked rock cliffs, sending loose boulders tumbling down the mountainside in avalanches that uprooted brush and trees.

The crews were in constant danger of being burned to death as the hurricane-like winds drove the fire in all directions, almost as if the monster wanted to be sure it killed everything in its proximity.

The fire was a dramatic leaven of natural instinct as two of the men were soon to discover. Jim Bushong and Herb Redtzke, college students and volunteer fighters, were forced by the crowning flames to retreat into the Wilson River at Devil's Ford. The two young men were immediately followed by a herd of black-tailed deer and a cougar, all bent on self-preservation and paying no attention to anything else. When the fires passed over, deer, men, and cat each went his own way, completely ignoring the others.

Refugees poured into Tillamook and Forest Grove with stories of disaster and narrow escapes. They told of livestock and deer encircled by the fire, frozen with fear and bleating as they roasted where they stood; of homes and barns burning while the owners stood by helplessly, or ran.

This one-time paradise for fishermen was turned into alkaline wallows. Dead fish floated in the superheated streams, their white bellies turned up to the sullen sky. The falling ash mixed with the water in the streams to become a sludgy mess

in which no fish could live. Thousands of bull-finches, sparrows, robins, and other birds flew out of the conflagration to land further north on the coast in Rockaway, desperately seeking relief from the dense, searing smoke.

Spot fires were popping up like fireflies. A flaming treetop dropped out of the murky sky into the Oregon-American timber holdings seven miles west of Vernonia and started another serious blaze. On the Nehalem River, near Nehalem Falls, more debris had set new fires, and on Rock Creek and Wolfe Creek new blazes were out of control. Spot fires became so numerous that it was impossible to keep track of them. Many reports were coming in now that communication was being re-established, but all the fire wardens could do was try to handle reports of the bigger fires. Small spots burned all through the dense forests of the Trask and Wilson, but men could not be sent in to the thickly-wooded areas for fear of being trapped if the cantankerous winds should shift.

The whirling winds drove the fire deeper into Yamhill County and the Floras timber holdings there. Owner Joe Floras set out from his company headquarters near Carlton with his own crew to fight for his economic livelihood. McMinnville officials were extremely worried about the city's water supply which was now being threatened. Townspeople could see the smoke plumes on the near horizon and as evening approached the sky was lighted by the twisting, dancing flames.

Governor Meier now issued an executive order closing down all logging activities in the four affected counties - Washington, Tillamook, Clatsop, and Yamhill. No logger could lift a hand except to fight the fires.

The Trask River fire was now correctly reported

41

 **DUDE'S COLISEUM**
TILLAMOOK

WEDNESDAY
THURSDAY   THE HOTTEST SHOW OF THE YEAR

The rarest bit of spice offered as screen entertainment
During the entire year

"WARRIOR'S HUSBAND"

Adapted from the book "Women of The Amazon" starring

ELISSA LANDI
DAVID MANNERS

You'll Laugh Loud, Long and Hearty   But you'll wonder where the screen is
going to stop   If you are fastidious don't see this   It's rare and racy   of course
All in fun   But it's plenty hot.

THE PREVIEW

BUSTER KEATON and JIMMY DURANTE

"WHAT! NO BEER?"

fifteen miles from Tillamook, and the fear of residents increased as they watched the flames move toward them from the mountain ridges. Virtually no business was conducted, and people milled about in the streets wondering at the speed and destructive force of this monster that was apparently set on destroying their city.

Ironically, the Tillamook Herald carried a full-page advertisement for the Coliseum Theater proclaiming that the Hottest Show of the Year "Warrior's Husband" was the feature that night. Tillamook had only to look toward the mountains to see the hottest show of the century!

This morning the *Portland Oregonian* said that there were fifteen hundred men fighting the fire and the wind was dying down. The front page carried a three-column cartoon farewell salute to the U.S.S. Constitution; bids were being called on the Wolfe Creek (Sunset) highway and floods in upper New York state were imperiling eight hundred people.

AUGUST 25, 1933

The great cloud hung suspended between heaven and the hell of the fire beneath. It grew larger by the hour, fed by smoke rising from below in a never-ending mass. Now it stretched from the outskirts of Portland westward as far as the eye could see over the ocean like a thick, black quilt completely blotting out the sun. The smoke covered cities and towns on the coast as far north as Astoria and to the south below Toledo, sixty miles from Tillamook.

Strong men quailed before the force and terror

of the flames. Some fled before the onslaught into creeks and rivers, others into the holocaust itself seeking safety in the burned-over areas behind the flames. Some merely sat down and wept in their exhaustion and frustration.

The Foss camp of the Hammond Lumber Company near Cook Creek was directly in the path of the flames as were camps eight and nine of the C.H. Wheeler Company north of Cochran, the Sam Feazel camp at Nehalem Falls, and the Marcum-Kellog camps on the Nehalem River; all were abandoned within hours.

The Vernonia fire had extended itself now to Spruce Run, a tributary of the Nehalem river, and new spot fires developed three miles south of Elsie. Farm families there were evacuated. Cochran, despite reports to the contrary, was still holding out although flames were marching toward it from both the north and south. This flourishing lumber town had been completely burned by forest fires the year before, and it was hoped what had been rebuilt would not perish also.

The historic Trask Toll House and stage stop had not burned as reported earlier, but the Orville Wilkes family, who lived there, was ordered to leave, thus accounting for all the ranch families residing in the Trask and Wilson watersheds. Summer home owners in this area frantically stripped their cabins of furnishings. The blaze had crowned again into virgin timber on the Whitney Company's holdings. The most alarming development of the morning was the spread of flames to the old Cedar Creek burn, twenty thousand acres of snags, that had been wiped out in 1918, and new growth in the slot north of the Wilson River which leads directly to the towns of Garibaldi and Bay City on Tillamook Bay.

51

A group of firefighters retreating from the revitalized Jordan Creek fire, twenty miles from Tillamook, reported that the Wilson River Lumber Company operations had been completely burned out, and that the Wilson fire was only about twelve miles from Tillamook.

The Rheer's place, which had been reported lost, was standing although several fishermen's cabins had burned. Fire crews again used it as a base from which to battle the east side of the fire.

Ranger Tom Stevens felt that the area around Saddle Mountain had cooled sufficiently to be entered. He left early in the afternoon for his lookout cabin and crows nest to survey the damage. The cabin had been completely destroyed, but the crows nest tree still stood.

Twenty men at the Wilson River Fish Hatchery reported that it looked like a hopeless fight but that they would stay on it as long as the ponds remained clear and pumping equipment held out.

The Wolfe Creek and Vernonia fires, which had started the day before, were about to merge and presented a grave threat to the Inman-Poulsen and Oregon-American lands. Several bridges and trestles on the Oregon-American logging railroad were destroyed and at Camp McGregor, in the mountains above Wolfe Creek, an engine with a string of flat cars was held in readiness, prepared for evacuation of loggers and their families.

The Vernonia fire, crowning before the east wind, swooped down on a forty-acre Inman-Poulsen mill pond, burned through a wooden dam, and rushed off completely uninhibited by the gush of the water stored behind the dam. An additional three hundred CCC tree troopers were rushed to Vernonia from their camps at Plaza, Parkdale, Bear Springs, and Summit to aid loggers in this fight.

53

Now the fire again made headlines in Portland. Two aerial photos of the cloud, covering one-half of the front page of the *Oregon Journal*, were accompanied by four stories devoted entirely to the fire. "SETTLERS FLEE FLAMES," "FALLING TREE KILLS YOUTH," "EERIE DRAMA OF WORLD AFLAME SEEN FROM AIR," "TREE FIRE SPREADS AROUND VERNONIA," read the black headlines.

AUGUST 26, 1933

With spot fires breaking out the last day and night, the inferno's front now stretched south from Grindstone Mountain and the Nestucca River through the canyons of the Trask, Wilson, and Salmonberry Rivers to the Nehalem in the north. A slight northerly shift of the wind was driving it deeper into Yamhill County closer to McMinnville to the southeast. Up north it was raging around Keasey, Vernonia, and Elsie and the eastern periphery was only eight miles from Forest Grove and the main fire fighting headquarters.

Ranchers and farmers on the Nehalem watched helplessly as their homes and outbuildings burned. A troop of Boy Scouts, camped at the Lukarilla ranch on the Nehalem, was forced to flee just after midnight as a gust of wind forced the fire up the river's canyon and almost into the camp. They were joined in their flight by four ranch families from the area who left their homes to avoid the same fiery, wind-whipped blast.

Elsie was being attacked on three sides and the shifting northerly wind reportedly was carrying the fire closer by the hour.

Near Vernonia the fire was marching to the sea, as resolutely as Sherman and his men, ravaging

everything in its path. In twenty-four hours it had covered an area five miles wide and twenty miles deep and now was momentarily marking time where Quarts Creek enters the Nehalem river. The town of Wheeler stood in its path, should it begin to move again.

Railroad construction crews were kept busy dousing tie fires along the Southern Pacific right of way. Despite their efforts, fires burned ties between Foss and Nehalem Falls and were burning also on the right of way near Enright.

The Wilson River fire was now reported within eight and one-half miles of Tillamook and still moving rapidly. The Trask fire was said to be about twelve miles from that city, but moving more slowly; it was burning timber around Skookum Lake, source of the Tillamook water supply. The Trask lookout reported the fire one-quarter of a mile from his station. He was told to "grab your gun and run." At the lookout atop Mt. Hebo, twelve miles to the south, John Ebinger reported before dawn that he could see the flames shooting out of the treetops to a height of sixteen hundred feet above the mountain. He told of the helplessness he felt as he watched new spot fires starting all through the countryside.

The entire fire front was sweeping generally south and west toward Tillamook and the coast in a huge horseshoe forty to fifty miles in length. Fire wardens estimated that it had traveled at least ten miles between midnight and dawn this morning. The speed of the fire was noted by the warden located eighteen miles up the Wilson from Tillamook. He was catching a much-needed nap when he was awakened at 2:00 a.m. by the roar of the approaching fire. At 5:00 a.m. it was in a canyon opposite his cabin howling and roaring like a storm

at sea. Two hours later the sound had completely subsided, the flames having advanced beyond hearing range.

The Wilson fire burned the Fall Creek bridge and the reconstructed Red bridge again this morning despite the efforts of the special crews sent to attempt to keep the bridges intact and the Wilson River road open. Food and equipment would now have to be mule-packed all the way from Tillamook to the crews on the western side of the fire, a distance of about eighteen miles.

Without warning, the wind shifted to the northwest and blew strongly once again, stopping the pell-mell run of the fire toward the sea. Now it turned back and began to burn the whole trees that had been killed but unburned in the frenetic march. At Nehalem Falls, the Feasle camp, which had been evacuated the day before, was leveled in moments.

Camp McGregor, the Oregon-American headquarters on Rock Creek near Keasey, which was bigger than many of the small towns in the four-county area, with bunk houses for two hundred loggers, homes for thirty married men, offices, and a company store, again was under serious threat of destruction. The women and children were loaded on the flat cars of the train that had been standing by for two days as the fire chewed its way into camp. Hooting forlornly, the engine, its spinning wheels seeking a grip on the rails, pulled the train out of the camp with agonizing slowness. The men left behind fought for every building in vain. A burning tree crashed across a pipeline leaving them without water. In an hour the camp and all its equipment were gone.

With the change of wind direction the villages of Wakefield, Maples, Enright, and Mayo were

Near Tillamook, apples baked on the trees.

alerted to the fire encroaching on them. About two hundred men, women, and children were preparing to leave. The canyon of the Salmonberry River was filled with smoke so thick that it was impossible to walk or see through the Southern Pacific tunnels. Visibility was down to two hundred feet. The railroad cancelled freight traffic over this line to concentrate all its efforts on fighting the fire.

The coastal town of Wheeler was now safe from the Nehalem fire which had changed direction. Elsie was completely surrounded and awaiting destruction, and blazing trees blocked the road in, making it impossible to get to the village to learn of its fate. A new fire in the Fisher Logging Company's holdings, twelve miles southeast of Astoria was moving steadily south and appeared to be about to join with the Vernonia fire. If this happened the fire would stretch from Astoria to the Nestucca River, a solid front of flames almost seventy miles long.

The town of Jewell was a partial victim of the Fisher fire. Several buildings in the town burned before the blaze could be brought under control and it seriously endangered the Clatskanie Fish Hatchery. Another new fire on the Lewis and Clark River was believed under control. The Nehalem fire, backtracking on itself, destroyed the Booth, Malarkey, and VanDuesen summer camps as well as five farms in the southwestern part of Clatsop county. Another new fire broke out on the East Side Logging Company lands in Clatsop County, raced twenty miles in a few hours to destroy the Oregon-American logging railroad, and burned to within three miles north of Cochran and west to Hamlet in the Nehalem valley.

Fire now moved to within a mile of the Forest Grove city limits, when flying brands landed in a

Mountains of desolation - the heart of Oregon's timber industry burned out.

61

stubble field on the Marion Tibbets farm setting the house, a threshing machine, outbuildings, and an automobile ablaze. Fire departments from Forest Grove and Cornelius managed to save the house, however, and kept the fire from spreading.

With the shift of the wind the people of Tillamook and the coast towns were enjoying a breathing spell from the smoke of the past few days but Portlanders were rubbing their smarting eyes as the cloud of smoke drifted over the Rose City and into the Willamette and Tualatin Valleys. The northwesterly winds carried the clouds of smoke as far south as Reno, Nevada, six hundred miles inland, where citizens complained of a haze and irritated eyes.

The Nestucca River lands were in the fire area now as the northwest winds chased the fire further southward. Two hundred men were sent into this fire to try to keep it from spreading through the headwaters of Beaver and Moon Creek and into the Siuslaw National Forest. Meadow Lake resorts were threatened and sportsmen all over Oregon were lamenting the loss of some of their favorite fishing and hunting grounds. Resort owners on the coast were complaining; the publicity given the fires in the past few days was keeping the tourists away, though the coast highway was open.

In the Wilson River area crews were still fighting desperately to save anything they could. A crew of ten men worked all night to save the ranger station on the Harris place, using wet sacks to beat out the sparks as they fell. Hero of that fight was Wilfred Pullem, an eighteen-year-old high school student, who stood all night over a spring near the ranger station and scooped up dishpans of water for the men to soak their sacks. This group had retreated more than twenty miles before the

fire in the last six days and the men were nearly exhausted from their flight.

The most heartening news of this day was *The Oregonian's* report that Joe Floras and his crew, who had almost been given up for lost in the Yamhill section of the fire, were reported safe and on their way home.

"FLAMES RAGE UNRESTRAINED," read the eight-column headline in the *Oregon Journal*. Three individual stories on the fire were headed "WINDS SEND BLAZE INTO YAMHILL," "TILLAMOOK PHONE LINE OUT," "EAST WIND INCREASES FIRE PERIL."

AUGUST 27, 1933

The Sunday morning papers proclaimed in two-inch high headlines that "FIRES SWEEP ON," while in actuality the wind had changed to the south and slackened, the humidity was rising, and fog had been moving over the burning timber lands all night.

The fire dropped to the ground and no longer raced through the treetops. The efforts of the men on the lines were finally beginning to take some effect, and crews were heartened at the weather bureau's prediction of rain. It had stayed on the ground for seven hours now and was not crowning or setting spot fires anywhere. It was not controlled, but at least it was where the men could get to it.

Animals driven half mad by the smoke and flames began to turn up in the more heavily inhabited areas around Forest Grove and Beaverton. An enraged black bear, singed by the fire, lumbered out of the woods a mile from Forest Grove and had to be shot by a farmer. Cougar tracks led from the fire

at Vernonia all the way to the tree-covered hills between Beaverton and Portland. He was not followed, for no one in his right mind wanted to tangle with a mad cougar looking for a place to hide from the unbearable heat and smoke. Frightened deer were seen in or near almost every village and town on the outer fringes of the fire.

A death-like calm settled over the western side of the fire and wardens at Three Rivers Ranger Station now concentrated on the Nestucca River fires, burning southward toward the Siuslaw National Forest. A battle plan called for more men to build fire lines from the headwaters of Beaver Creek, Moon Creek, East Creek down Bear Creek to the Nestucca. Another line would run eastward from the Nestucca to Bald Mountain and Meadow Lake. Secondary lines would be set up at the river itself and on Testament Creek and Willamina Creek. If the fire got beyond those lines it would have a strangle hold on the National Forest. Ironically, the efforts of the fire generals were now hampered considerably by a complete lack of wind, for smoke from spot fires hung over the main lookout on Mt. Hebo. Visibility was down to one hundred feet.

Portland and the entire Tualatin Valley to the south were shrouded in smoke this day. Without the east wind to carry the smoke to the coast, the clouds were drifting inland where they would hover for two days.

Previously unreported spot fires had burned Hamlet Camp near Humbug Mountain and were burning on Sweethome Creek near Hamlet. Another was reported on Deer Creek near McMinnville and men were sent to trail it. "Probable light rains" were predicted by the weather bureau and the hopes of men on the lines continued to rise.

67

The people of Wheeler, with blazes within three and one-half miles of their town, were overjoyed to report misty rain moving into the area, their first sign of relief. Rain was reported also at Cloverdale on the south side of the fire.

AUGUST 28, 1933

The war of man versus the elements of nature was two weeks old. Light rain, mist, and fog moved slowly over the entire fire area. The wind had died to a breathless calm, and the blaze was smothering slowly. Loggers, CCC tree troopers, and forestry officials began to contain the flaming monster that had ruled their lives for fourteen days and nights.

Regions that had cooled enough for human habitation were opened as soon as possible for former residents to pack in to assess the damage to their homes and property.

Elsie was found very much alive, refuting earlier reports of the town's destruction. It was one of several islands in the forest surviving the sea of flames that had engulfed most of the area. To this day, thirteen thousand-odd acres of tall timber stand in mute mockery of the inferno, including forest monarchs at Gobblers Knob, Windy Point, Hembre Ridge, and the west side of South Saddle Mountain.

Women and children in Elsie had done their jobs well, forming bucket brigades and using wet sacks to beat out hot sparks, dousing the flame brands that settled like unwelcome guests within the village.

Remarkable tales floated from camp to camp, much as had the burning brands during the height of the fire. Two women, wives of forest wardens, refused to leave the fire area when the families were evacuated. One of them remained in her cab-

in on the Trask River with her two-year-old baby and the family dog. Engrossed in household chores the mother suddenly missed the youngster. Rushing into the clearing surrounding the cabin she saw her child about to be embraced by a huge black bear. She screamed, the dog barked, and both charged the bear. The bear immediately retreated, preferring the flaming forest to a screaming woman and a barking dog.

A lonely cat, left behind when a family was forced to leave, was found alive at the site of an old Trask homestead. Her kittens had burned, as had all the livestock when the old landmark, with its barns and stables, bowed to the flames.

The Wilson River road was littered with the carcasses of deer that had been overcome by the flames and smoke while attempting to flee. One was found impaled on the limb of a fallen tree. Apparently blinded by smoke and terrified with fear, it had charged into the limb, piercing his body from chest to hindquarters. Another lay crushed by a fallen snag. Whole herds were huddled in groups where their charred bodies had dropped in midflight, their faces pointed to the west and safety. Does picked their way through the charred mass of rubble, once their home, looking forlornly for fawns that had become lost in the smoke and confusion. Mother bears and cougars sniffed around burned-out caves, hopefully seeking some signs of cubs that had been lost in the panic of flight from the flames.

Wildlife exponents were incensed. Letters were written to the editors of every newspaper in the Willamette Valley and on the coast proclaiming a need for close supervision of The Burn to deter hunters and poachers. The wildlife, driven from the area, had to be protected against unregulated hunt-

The Trask homestead was one of several historic landmarks that fell before the relentless flames.

71

ing until such time as the herds of deer and elk could propagate and the forest could grow up enough to provide adequate food and protection for both old and young animals.

Tillamook reported a serious milk shortage. Cows were unable to graze on pastures covered by ashes up to three feet deep.

A mountainous task now faced the country road crews. It was estimated that it would take two weeks to clear the Wilson River Road for travel. Red Bridge at Illingsworths could be repaired quickly if the fog and mist held but there was still the Jordan Creek, Fall Creek, and numerous other small bridges to put back in shape or replace.

According to scouts in the burn, when the roads and bridges were open again, the summer residents would be in for a shock, for there were few homes that had not been completely destroyed. Those that were not totally ruined were severely damaged.

The inferno now was controlled on all fronts, with the fog and mist being a key factor in holding it within bounds. Excess CCC boys and volunteers were being sent home. Forest wardens were wary, however, and continued to build trails, setting up secondary defense lines should the moist air disappear and the wind rise again. According to forestry officials, it would take an eight-inch rainfall to douse the fire completely.

The blanket of fog and mist continued for more than a week. Slowly, but surely, the fires were smothered. Forestry officials began to feel better.

The Trask River fire, burning south toward Mt. Hebo, uncovered the evidence to support a legend that had been prevalent on the Oregon coast for a century or more. The story concerned a great forest fire that covered thirty-five hundred square miles and burned steadily for four years. It was said to

Heavy undergrowth in the coastal range made trailing the fire an extreme effort for the fire crews.

have burned so rapidly at times that wildlife were forced to take refuge in the Pacific surf and it was reported to have destroyed the world's largest and finest stand of Douglas fir.

Forestry officials did not doubt the authenticity of the legend as far as the magnitude of the fire. The evidence uncovered by the Trask blaze bears out the size of the fire and the area covered. The possibility of its burning for four years was officially considered doubtful since the fog, mist, and heavy rains that frequent the area would make a fire of this duration a near impossibility.

However, one year later, August 1, 1934, scouts exploring the Tillamook Burn for salvageable timber, found fire still burning inside a giant white fir snag!

"HENRY FORD, KEY TO NRA PACT," made headlines this morning. The mist in the burn rated only a column head, but the newspapers did run a feature article on the old Wilson River Road and the part it had played in the fire. The article claimed that the road had been conceived by fiends and executed by mountain goats when describing the movements of hundreds of trucks and thousands of men over its dizzying curves, narrow, tortuous grades and impossible inclines. According to the papers, many people had said that the road was impassable, having been let go to ruin during the past twenty-five years. Forestry officials, having seen its usefulness the past two weeks, tended to disagree.

SEPTEMBER 5, 1933.

RAIN...A hard pelting rain that lasted for days. The forest wardens got their wishes and more. The fire was out. All that was left was a charred ruin. The terror of the flames was over now. The horror

75

engulfed the state like a black shroud. An area about one-half the size of Rhode Island was a wasteland.

Officially the Tillamook Burn included the Trask River fire, The Wilson River fire, the Jordan and Gales Creek fires, and the Nehalem and Salmonberry River fires. Three hundred and eleven thousand smoldering acres of dead forest. Two hundred and forty thousand of those acres had burned in that terrible twenty hours of August 24-25.

During the same period sixty thousand acres had burned in the Wolfe Creek-Vernonia fire and another forty thousand had burned when the Fisher fire stormed down toward the Tillamook Burn from Astoria. These were not in the official Tillamook Burn. Nevertheless, they burned at the same time and were in part responsible for the pall depressing the people of the state. Three hundred eleven thousand acres plus the additional one hundred thousand acres totals four hundred and eleven thousand acres, or more than six hundred square miles. Over thirteen billion board feet of timber had been killed. The heart of the greatest timber producing state in the nation burned out in fourteen days. Why? Greed and carelessness. Square miles, acres, board feet, numbers — figures that all added up to one word, disaster. Disaster to the people, disaster to the logging operators, disaster to the state, and even the nation.

What did these figures mean to the people directly involved?

According to Sinclair A. Wilson, senior forest economist, Pacific Northwest Forest Experiment Station, thirteen billion board feet of timber standing tall and green instead of blackened and smoldering was worth $275,000,000 in 1933. If cut, it would have kept fourteen thousand loggers

and sawyers working forty hours a week fifty-two weeks a year for six years. In terms of wages, this would amount to $3,000,000,000 to these people. It represented the production of all the lumber, shingle, lath, and pulpwood mills in the United States for a full year in the early 1930's.

With the aftermath came despair—the fire enemy had been defeated, but no one had been the victor. Tillamook County faced beggardom. The burned timber represented $400,000 in taxes, almost one-half of the county tax revenue for the year at the current logging rates. The officials saw their county facing bankruptcy.

The logging operators, with their railroads burned, their equipment destroyed or stranded in a forest of blackened, unsaleable snags could see financial ruin written in indelible charcoal across the face of those four hundred thousand odd acres. Over a million dollars in equipment was ruined or stranded. The timber owners and mill operators had lost much but for every dollar they lost the public stood to lose five in money that would not find its way into the economy.

Frank Palmer was dead!

The usual belief that a forest fire consumes the trees, reducing them to a pile of ashes, is untrue. Growing timber, particularly big timber, is killed by fire. Stripped of its leaves or needles, denuded of its bark and limbs, a dead snag soon becomes prey to insects that bore into the heartwood allowing disease and decay to enter and finish the job. No mill, of course, will buy defective or rotten logs... and so the dead trees remain, grisly tombstones marking the many deaths of the burned forest.

Timber cruisers, playing medical examiners for the logging operators, went into the Tillamook Burn even before the snags had stopped smolder-

ing. Their reports were more heartening than expected. A considerable amount of sound, although dead, trees remained. Salvage, however, was a big undertaking, particularly difficult because of the equipment losses. Salvage, to be worthwhile, had to be done soon, and at great risk for the operators, for there was no ready market for burned timber.

To some owners, logging the timber in The Burn seemed like a hopeless task. Railroads had to be rebuilt. Equipment had to be overhauled or replaced. It would mean a tremendous investment with little or no promise of return.

Many looked upon salvage as unprofitable and turned away from the possibility. More than one hundred and twenty-five thousand acres of salvageable timber were abandoned and allowed to revert to the county for unpaid taxes. Legal complications tied up these lands for more than six years. According to the experts, this was time enough for insects and disease to do their deadly work.

After a thorough survey, the more farsighted of the major logging companies pooled their resources for the greatest timber-saving operation in the history of lumbering. At best they had until 1940 to get the timber out of the burned area, according to foresters.

While these operators were meeting to discuss their plans for salvage, a few of the independent loggers were active. Three of these concerns owned mills as a part of their overall operations. Their alternatives were clear: log The Burn or close up. Fortunately, they chose to go back to logging.

Within three months after the fire, even before many snags had cooled enough to cut, the sounds of saw, axe, and donkey engine were heard again in The Burn. It was unlike any logging operation the men had ever seen. They worked in soot and ashes up to their knees at times. Nowhere was there the fresh smell of the forest. No rabbits and chipmunks skittered through the thickets—there were no thickets, just as there were no forest denizens. All that was left were the men, their equipment, and the black-encrusted skeletons that made up the crop they were trying so desperately to harvest. At the end of the day it was not pitch the men had to scrub off. It was soot. Soot in their clothes, soot on their bodies, soot in their eyes, noses, and ears. By the end of a work shift, the loggers resembled a gang of coal miners leaving the pits.

The independents logged out of desperation, but other firms had formed a company for the sole purpose of logging The Burn. Tillamook County cooperated to the extent of cancelling the usual taxes on the land. Instead, an agreement was worked out so that in lieu of straight property taxes the loggers would pay a tax of five cents per thousand board feet on any timber logged and sold.

The new company, Consolidated Logging Company, could log without fear of mills refusing to buy. It had its own mills.

Now the race against time was on. Gandy dancers went into The Burn to repair trestles and track, and did not come out again until they had laid the company's new steel to where the Great Northern Railroad's spur line from Portland ended at the foot of the coast range near Gales Creek, the starting point of the fire. It was a four percent grade that branched out on both sides into the charred snags of The Burn. Tree fallers moved in right after the railroaders and as soon as the steel was tied up the balance of the loggers, with over $4,000,000 in new equipment, plunged into the charred forest for the struggle against time, insects, and rot.

Every possible means of getting the timber cut

and out was used. Bulldozers sliced dirt roads out of the mountainsides; trucks following close behind groaned their way up the rough grades. By June, 1934, this hi-grade operation was in full swing. Only number-one timber was to be taken. Nothing under twenty-four inches in diameter was to be cut; this operation was to salvage the big ones. Snags eight to ten feet around and one hundred and fifty to two hundred feet tall were first choice of the fallers. The buckers sawed them into lengths ranging from seventy to ninety feet, and the steam donkeys dragged them to the landings. Long trains loaded with coal-black logs chuffed out of the mountains, dumped their loads for the Great Northern and Southern Pacific to pick up and snorted back up the grades for another load. The log dumps of the Willamette and Tualatin Rivers and the holding ponds of mills on the coast were blackened by the timber.

The economy of the country was on the upswing. Lumber was more and more in demand. Beneath the charred exterior of the giants many hundreds of thousands of board feet of sound lumber were hidden. Independent mills soon discovered this and the demand for the black skeletons rose.

In the next six years the independents and Consolidated logged off one hundred million board feet of usable timber.

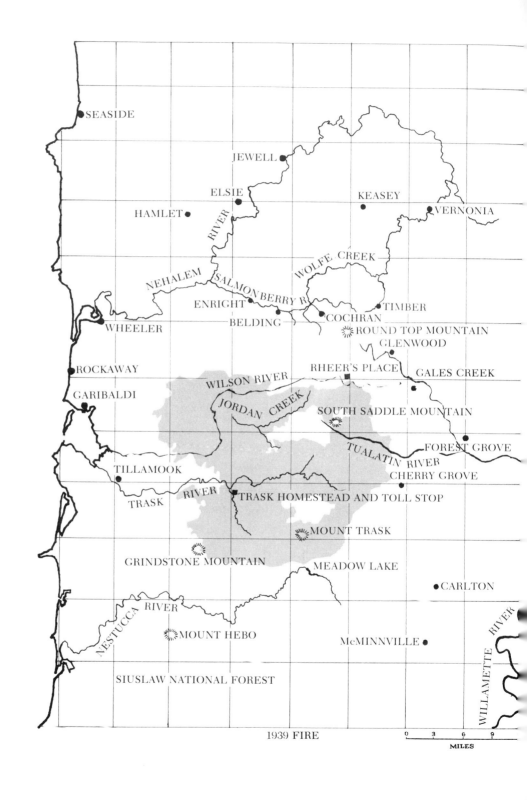

SEASIDE

JEWELL

ELSIE

HAMLET

KEASEY

VERNONIA

NEHALEM RIVER

WOLFE CREEK

SALMONBERRY R.

ENRIGHT

BELDING

COCHRAN

TIMBER

ROUND TOP MOUNTAIN

WHEELER

GLENWOOD

ROCKAWAY

WILSON RIVER

RHEER'S PLACE

GALES CREEK

GARIBALDI

JORDAN CREEK

SOUTH SADDLE MOUNTAIN

FOREST GROVE

TUALATIN RIVER

TILLAMOOK

CHERRY GROVE

TRASK

RIVER

TRASK HOMESTEAD AND TOLL STOP

MOUNT TRASK

GRINDSTONE MOUNTAIN

MEADOW LAKE

CARLTON

NESTUCCA RIVER

MOUNT HEBO

McMINNVILLE

WILLAMETTE RIVER

SIUSLAW NATIONAL FOREST

1939 FIRE

0   3   6   9

MILES

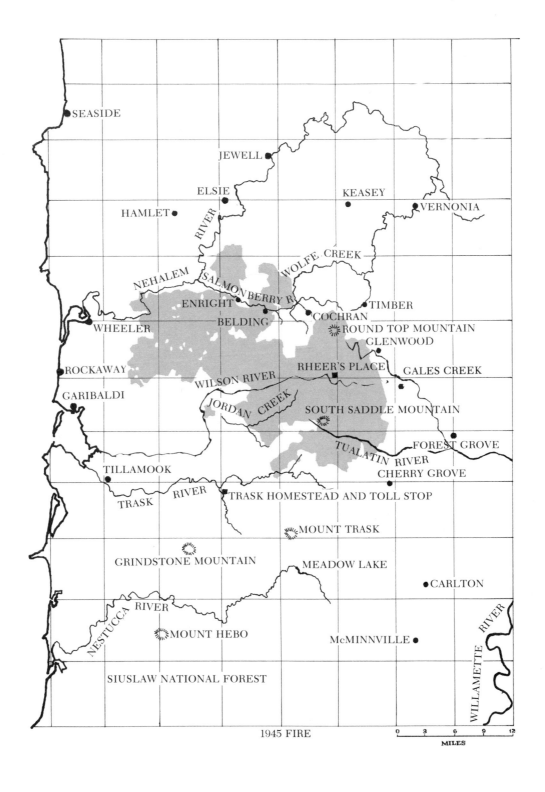

SEASIDE

JEWELL

ELSIE

KEASEY

HAMLET

VERNONIA

NEHALEM RIVER

WOLFE CREEK

SALMONBERRY R.

ENRIGHT

TIMBER

BELDING

COCHRAN

WHEELER

ROUND TOP MOUNTAIN

GLENWOOD

ROCKAWAY

RHEER'S PLACE

GALES CREEK

WILSON RIVER

GARIBALDI

JORDAN CREEK

SOUTH SADDLE MOUNTAIN

TUALATIN RIVER

FOREST GROVE

TILLAMOOK

CHERRY GROVE

TRASK RIVER

TRASK HOMESTEAD AND TOLL STOP

MOUNT TRASK

GRINDSTONE MOUNTAIN

MEADOW LAKE

CARLTON

NESTUCCA RIVER

MOUNT HEBO

McMINNVILLE

WILLAMETTE RIVER

SIUSLAW NATIONAL FOREST

1945 FIRE

0   3   6   9   12

MILES

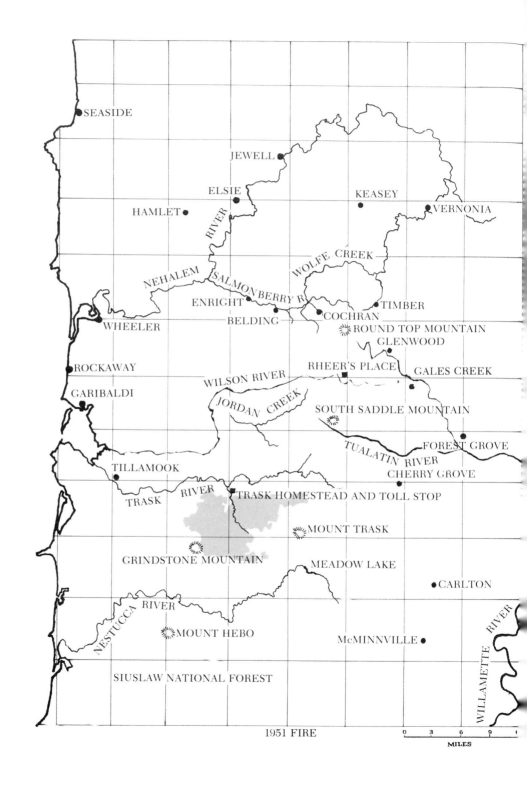

SEASIDE

JEWELL

ELSIE

KEASEY

HAMLET

VERNONIA

RIVER

WOLFE CREEK

NEHALEM

SALMONBERRY R.

ENRIGHT

TIMBER

BELDING

COCHRAN

WHEELER

ROUND TOP MOUNTAIN

GLENWOOD

ROCKAWAY

WILSON RIVER

RHEER'S PLACE

GALES CREEK

GARIBALDI

JORDAN CREEK

SOUTH SADDLE MOUNTAIN

FOREST GROVE

TUALATIN RIVER

CHERRY GROVE

TILLAMOOK

TRASK RIVER

TRASK HOMESTEAD AND TOLL STOP

TRASK

MOUNT TRASK

GRINDSTONE MOUNTAIN

MEADOW LAKE

CARLTON

NESTUCCA RIVER

MOUNT HEBO

McMINNVILLE

WILLAMETTE RIVER

SIUSLAW NATIONAL FOREST

1951 FIRE

0   3   6   9

MILES

EPILOGUE

"Fire, fire in Gales Creek Canyon!" The date was August 1, 1939, and history was repeating itself. A careless contractor, ignition, and flames again roared through the snags. The fire started in Gales Creek Canyon, in almost the same place as the first Burn, and rekindled more than two hundred thousand acres of the 1933 Tillamook Burn, plus an additional twenty thousand acres of green timber. It burned south over Grindstone mountain, down the Wilson and Trask rivers to within four and one-half miles of Tillamook, and east to within a mile of Cherry Grove. Trask mountain burned completely. On the northern perimeter, the firefighters managed to contain it within the old Burn area, but it seared several of the green islands within the old Burn including the north side of Hembre Ridge.

The pattern of this fire was much like that of its infamous predecessor. Whipped by a vicious wind, it rampaged through the forests at will. Fire brands dropped into the Floras holdings again, where a crew coming off the Hoot Owl shift at Camp Two was almost trapped and their camp was reduced to rubble. Dwayer Logging Company lost five million board feet of cut logs and five steam donkeys when its camp burned. Trask-Willamette's camp was wiped out and Oregon-American took a terrible beating, losing five railroad bridges, fourteen million board feet of dressed logs, fifteen steam donkeys and two locomotives. The Stimson Company was ready this time. Its men managed to save donkeys, tools, machinery, and all other equipment by moving it out of the fire zone on trains. Floras was not as fortunate. Three days after it started, the fire, as it moved east, devoured what remained of the green Floras holdings, and then

demolished the headquarters camp. Again, men watched helplessly as the flames rampaged up the draw in which the camp was located, swallowed up the commissary, bunkhouses, and all the equipment. Over the roar of the flames could be heard the exploding of the dynamite caches, placed at random for safety's sake throughout the camp. When it was over, Floras was wiped out. All trestles were burned, and every piece of equipment was destroyed or stranded in The Burn. Nothing was left with which to try to salvage more timber from The Burn.

Smoke boiled up over the peaks of the coast range and ashes and brands rained down on the surrounding countryside. Fire-litter once more showered Tillamook and northern Oregon coastal cities. The author witnessed this fire, as a Boy Scout at Camp Meriwether on the coast just below Tillamook. Ashes, needles, and debris fell from the sky for days. The sun's rays were ghost-like filtered by the dense smoke. At night the sky glowed with an eerie light. The senior scouts and their leaders were recruited for the firelines, much to the envy of the younger scouts who yearned for the adventure of being on the front with the older boys. The young scouts, however, remained in camp where they put out hot sparks and firebrands with wet sacks.

The fire was almost as bad as in 1933. The snags of the first burn blazed with unquenchable fury and when the wind blew it played hopscotch again with the flames. When the wind decreased, the fire dropped to the ground, where fireweed, the first ground cover to grow after the initial burn, provided tinder to continue the inferno. Four thousand men struggled four weeks to get the blaze under control, but not until the rains came on Aug-

ust 28 did they finally conquer it. One-half million dollars had been spent just in fighting the fire.

Newspapers treated the fire differently this time. It made headlines almost every day, and for almost a full month little else received space on the front pages.

Many logging operators were burned out; others simply got out of the timber industry. Consolidated Logging Company was in control of more than one hundred thousand acres in this devil's forest, and the need for the seared giants was increasing, as the war in Europe and the American preparedness program began making great demands on the forest products industry. America had become "The Arsenal of Democracy," the warehouse of everything the beseiged nations of Europe needed to fight against Hitler and fascism.

The shipyards being built in Portland and Vancouver, Washington were in need of timber; timber to build wharfs, warehouses, and ship-ways. The Tillamook Burn had the lumber to supply these needs, but after the 1933 Burn, forestry experts had predicted that disease and rot would make the killed trees unusable after six or seven years. Loggers in the neighboring states of Washington and California took another look at The Burn, for here was cheap timber with a ready market. Timber cruisers examined the blackened snags again and found for the most part good, saleable timber. The experts had been wrong.

When the out-of-state logging companies began to work The Burn, interest in the area became keen for other Oregon loggers, for if there was cheap timber close to the market, they wanted to be in on the operation, too. Activity increased at the Tillamook County Court House, where permits were issued to clean out the snags. County of-

After several close escapes in the earlier fire, the Floras Logging Camp was burned out in the 1939 fire.

ficials were more than ready to deal, for they recognized that prosperity depended upon marketing the dead trees, and seven years of reduced activity in the county's forests had seriously threatened the county economy. Tillamook County set a tax price of $1 per thousand board feet on Douglas fir cut and sold, a considerable increase from the five cents per thousand that had been charged the loggers the past seven years. Nevertheless, the price was fair for both the county and the loggers.

Manpower now was the big problem. The shipyards, with their fantastic wages, no winter shutdowns, and three shifts a day, had lured hundreds of fallers, buckers, and scalers to Portland and Vancouver. A shortage of equipment hampered operations in the forests, too, for the war that had created the sudden demand for timber also made machinery almost impossible to get. The loggers had to make do with the equipment they had and what they could salvage from the old equipment in The Burn. When the United States entered the war the situation was worse; men answered draft calls, and equipment became impossible to get, yet the demands for the giants increased. The loggers now began to take out the smaller trees in The Burn, and even these were acceptable to the log-hungry buyers.

By 1942, The Burn had become a powder keg. Men, when they could be had, worked around the clock, their clattering machinery held together with bailing wire and spit. Dry weather made the fire danger acute during the summer months, and the many loggers with untrustworthy equipment working without a letup enhanced this danger even more. Wardens were on their guard, for another fire now could hamper seriously the war effort as well as destroy any chance of future

The Tillamook Burn in 1958, twenty-five years after the first fire.

93

salvage of the timber.

The fire wardens were not the only ones with their eyes on The Burn. In the summer of 1942, the Japanese High Command was studying the forests of the Pacific Northwest and their history of fire. The Japanese recognized what a big fire in the coast range would do to the war production, and knew that a series of fires would pull men off the production lines. A constant danger of fire, whether real or imagined, would create havoc among the people, also.

The High Command was quick to act. In August, 1942, the submarine I-25 left Yokohama harbor bound for the coast of Oregon. Beneath her steel deckplates was a disassembled Zero float plane. During the inky blackness of night on September 8, the I-25 surfaced silently off Cape Blanco, where the crew assembled the Zero and loaded it with incendiary bombs. The mission of the Zero's pilot was to drop incendiaries on the forest of the Oregon coast, let his plane, with its Rising Sun markings, be seen and, if possible, escape to sea and the I-25. The pilot accomplished his assignment, but the blaze started by his bombs was controlled immediately by alert foresters. No one realized a hostile bomber had caused the fire until bomb fragments, with their Japanese markings, were discovered in the area where the fire started. Some people had seen the plane, too, but none believed that it really was Japanese.

The Zero made it safely back to the I-25 and was stored below again. Ten days later the submarine surfaced again off the Oregon coast, and the plane roared into the early morning sky. This time the bombs fell on the Siuslaw National Forest, just south of the Tillamook Burn. The bombs did no appreciable damage, but the pilot, on his return

Silhouetted against a blackened stump is Fireweed, the first ground cover to return to a burned area after a fire.

95

DEDICATED
TO THOSE
WHO DIED HERE
MAY 5 1945
BY
JAPANESE
BOMB EXPLOSION

THE ONLY PLACE
ON THE
AMERICAN CONTINENT
WHERE DEATH RESULTED
FROM ENEMY ACTION
DURING WORLD WAR II

home, was promoted for his daring and heroism.

While the I-25 was conducting its mission, the Japanese were planning top-secret Project V-1. This ingenious plan was to release thousands of thirty to forty-foot balloons, made of rice paper and covered with wax, which would drift high in the jet stream from Japan, Formosa, and the Kurile Islands, over Alaska and down the coast of Canada to bomb the forests of Washington, Oregon, and northern California. If effective, the bombs not only would start fires but would panic the population of America's coastal states.

Each gas-filled balloon carried two incendiary bombs, one fragmentation bomb, and a timing device designed to allow the gas to escape after fifty hours of flight, the amount of time estimated to complete the drift to the coast where the balloons would drop in the forests. By December, 1944, Project V-1 was ready to execute. Nine thousand balloons were sent up from Tokyo and another sixty thousand reportedly were released from Formosa and the Kurile Islands during the next several months. Of these, only about one thousand actually reached the United States, and only a few were known to have exploded. One damaged a high tension power line leading to the Hanford Atomic works, another went off in a farmer's field fifty miles east of Portland, starting a small grass fire. A third exploded in the middle of a group of picnickers on Weyerhaeuser Company property near Bly, in Southern Oregon, killing six persons. These were the only casualties in the continental United States attributed directly to an enemy action during World War II.

Twelve counties in Oregon reported balloon landings. One was reported near Seattle, several in northern California, and one landed in the Mare

This monument, on Weyerhaeuser lands near Bly, Oregon, stands in tribute to the only persons in the continental United States whose deaths were attributed to direct enemy action in World War II. Six died from the explosion of a Japanese balloon bomb.

97

Island Naval Complex in San Francisco Bay. Several drifted far inland, including one that landed in Michigan and another in Texas. Project V-1, another of man's attempts to destroy the giants was a two-year, $200,000,000 failure, and was discontinued shortly before the war ended.

Despite bombers and balloons, salvage in the Tillamook Burn had gone on and the charcoaled snags continued to pour into the mill ponds in the Willamette Valley. But on July 10, 1945, the loggers themselves did what the Japanese had failed to do. The six-year curse struck again—the fire-monster was loose in The Burn once more. No one knows for sure how it started, but this time, as before, a fire ignited in Gales Creek Canyon and the whole of South Saddle Mountain was ablaze in a very short time. Thousands of loggers, servicemen, shipyard workers, and other volunteers were recruited to fight the third battle of The Burn. It was a repeat of the two previous big fires, an inferno that rushed out of control to kill more green timber as well as strike again the twice-devastated snags.

The fire burned east to within a mile of Glenwood and two miles of Gales City to the north. All of Round Top Mountain was burned as were Rogers Peak, Pinochle Peak, and Buck Mountain. The town of Belding was surrounded as the fire moved farther north, where it jumped the Salmonberry River, climbed Bare Mountain and finally stopped on the crest of Four Seven Ridge. To the west and south, the fire stayed within the boundaries of the original Tillamook Burn. Again, an area of more than two hundred thousand acres was aflame in the original Burn, as well as about thirty thousand acres of green timber.

After its first rush, when it grew to a width of fifty miles in six days, the fire became a slow,

Trucks replaced trains in The Burn after World War II.

99

wandering blaze, with little jumping or spotting but a steady, creeping death for the giants.

Thirty-five hundred men battled the conflagration, but they could not seem to get it under control. They were disorganized, discouraged, and without direction. Crews would rush from place to place where they would unpack their tools, fight for awhile, pack up, and rush off again.

On July 26, the Tillamook Burn claimed its second life. A logger, Joe Dillish, was crushed by a falling snag as he attempted to clear a trail around the fire.

The newspapers made much of this fire, too. From July 11 to August 5 the fire made the front pages every day but on August 6, the atomic bomb was dropped on Hiroshima, and the fire became secondary once again to the war and the Japanese surrender.

After burning for more than eight weeks, the fire was conquered finally by rain.

Salvage of the trees continued in The Burn, but now it was a different operation. The equipment was changing and so were the men.

No more would the huff and snort of locomotives and steam donkeys be heard in The Burn, as gasoline and diesel fuel provided energy for the job. Now, more than ever, it was hurry, hurry, hurry. The power saw became the prime tool of the fallers, ripping out more of the giants before the predicted decay could set in. Still the demand for timber rose. Veterans, returning from the war, got married and they sought housing for their families. Industry, fat from war contracts, wanted to expand. Building was at its zenith and mills were becoming less and less particular about the grade of log they would accept.

As the loggers came back from military service,

A fawn orphaned by the fire is adopted by the soldiers from Fort Lewis who helped fight the 1945 conflagration.

101

shipyards, and defense plants, they found this new way of logging to their liking. Two men could pool their mustering-out pay or shipyard savings, buy an old engine that could be converted to use as a donkey, a second-hand truck, bulldozer and power saws, get a stumpage lease or contract and they were in business. They might not get rich, although some of them made much money, but they were their own bosses and they liked it.

The blackened crags, gullies, and mountains re-sounded to the staccato bark of the engines and the whine of the power saws. Oregon's highways were crowded with log trucks; up to three thousand truckloads of charcoal-coated logs made their way to dumps at mills, rivers, and rail heads weekly. The Southern Pacific was forced to hook as many as seven engines to a train to pull the loaded log cars over the mountains from the Tillamook side of The Burn every evening.

Sightseers, tourists, and traveling men cursed the truckers. Log rigs were everywhere, often popping out of unmarked side roads or groaning slowly up the steep grades of the Wilson River and Wolfe Creek highways. A trip to the coast was an endurance test of a driver's nerves and sense of humor when locked in a string of the creeping be-hemoths of the road.

The demand for the snags from The Burn contin-ued, and more and more leniency in quality was allowed. The number of outfits, big and small, working The Burn rose from fewer than fifty be-fore and during the war to more than two hundred by 1950. The loggers needed much know-how, a lot of jury-rigs, Rube Goldburg contraptions, common sense, and good old American ingenuity, but in twenty-five years, they had logged off most of the salvageable timber in The Burn.

A seedling nursery at Corvallis, Oregon is one of the many sources of plants that have been used for reforestation of The Burn.

Then came the reloggers, who were even less particular than those who had gone before. If a snag or windfall was anywhere near sound, short or tall, thin or thick, they took it. At this stage, the under-supplied mills did not care, as long as the timber did not foul the machinery.

Six years had passed, and the ravaged area had had no fire. But on July 20, 1951, with the temperature hovering near one hundred degrees, a logging gang blasted a treetop to make a spar tree, and sparks from the blast started a new fire. The Red Curse had struck once more.

Soon the whole of Elkhom Canyon on the North Fork of the Trask River was ablaze, and the fire roared through the snags and fireweed to wipe out Ginsberg Point again, climbed Gold Peak, and moved south as far as Grindstone Mountain. To the west it climbed Edwards Butte and to the north it burned as far as the village of Trask.

This time the fire wardens were ready. The alarm had hardly sounded when crews with bulldozers and other heavy equipment moved over the fire roads into the path of the inferno. Rainmakers were on hand, but they did not get a chance to prove themselves. On July 24, the fire had been trailed and by the next day it was under control. It had burned over twenty thousand acres in those few days; fortunately, almost all of the territory afire was within the boundaries of the previous burns.

Salvageable timber in The Burn diminished slowly; most of the dead trees remaining showed signs of greater decay and defect, and they were not many more decent logs left. Simultaneously, the demand for timber from The Burn waned. The post-war building boom had leveled off and the need for logs of any grade was coming to an end. Soon the

105

angry whine of the chain saw, the snort of the "cat", and the grumble of the laden trucks began to fade from The Burn. The giants had had their day. They had proved their worth. They had been ravaged three times by the greatest conflagrations in any forest, had been derided as a gigantic stand of useless snags, yet had gone to war and had contributed to one of the greatest periods in the nation's economy. More than seven billion board feet of timber had been salvaged. This was an enviable record for forest lands that once had been considered a multi-billion dollar ghost.

Man was not through with The Burn. He had made it what it was now he would remake it into what it had been. He would pour millions of dollars and hundreds of thousands of hours into restoring this devastated land. He would make it a paradise for outdoorsmen once more. He would nurture seedlings until they became monarchs. He would put giants there again.

Both private industry and the general public took it as a personal challenge to see that the forest should flourish again in the four counties — bigger, greener, and more lush than ever.

The fires of 1939 and 1945 had severely damaged any seed crop that might have survived the original fire and so it became vogue for garden clubs, civic and social groups, school children, and scout troops to organize tree planting expeditions in The Burn. Forestry officials not only welcomed the efforts of all groups but furnished seedlings from the state nurseries, showed how and where to plant them, and energetically supported continued reforestation.

Not enough words exist to praise the efforts of the Oregon State Forestry Department. One hundred and sixty thousand acres of The Burn have

107

been reseeded or replanted to trees since the state foresters became the prime movers in The Burn's rehabilitation. Over seven hundred miles of fire roads have been built for fire protection and forest management and maintenance. By 1972 the job will be completed and by the year 2000 the first crop will be ready to harvest. The cost: ten and one-half million dollars. The expected return: two-hundred million dollars!

Timber production is only one of the benefits to be expected from the rebirth of The Burn. Watershed protection, fish and game propagation, and recreational facilities for the rapidly growing population can also be numbered among the benefits of the multi-use policy planned for this once-devastated area.

Since 1950, when this epilogue in the history of The Burn started, volunteer groups alone have planted over two hundred and fifty thousand seedlings. Private industry has made massive contributions to the restoration and revitalization of The Burn. Georgia-Pacific, Boise Cascade, Weyerhaeuser, Crown Zellerbach and all the great names in Northwest timber products have established tree farms and research centers in or near The Burn to develop or refine new concepts of logging, forest production, and forest care and maintenance. The private companies have worked cooperatively with state and national foresters in these studies.

Deer now roam through the snags and new growth; rabbits and squirrels skitter through the underbrush; even bears and cougars have come back. The streams are alive with fish again. On weekends, sportsmen's cars are parked at the roadside near every creek and river. The Oregon State Game Commission has worked continuously to accomplish this rebirth of the forest's wildlife. It has taken much effort on their part for this area to even begin to regain the wildlife population of the past. Hundreds of thousands of fingerlings have been planted in the streams of The Burn. Whole herds of deer have been transported to the area from all over the state. The repopulation and reforestation has been, and will continue to be, an incredible effort of marked success.

Drive through The Burn in the spring. Amid the old, blackened relics of the past, one can see new shoots springing up, coaxed into life by the warm rains and spring sunshine. In the summer, marvel at the recovery the forest has made. The young trees in full foliage standing beside the dark-gutted specters are a jolting contrast and all who pass by are reminded of the beauty that once stood there; the beauty that is rising to stand again. The time to enjoy The Burn the most is in the fall, when mother nature illuminates the leaves. With the dark green of the firs and the gray and black of the snags as a background, a riot of color is draped over the entire area. The valleys, hills, and peaks are decked out in glories such as Solomon had never seen. Fall in the Tillamook Burn is a sight no one should miss, if he has to travel a thousand miles. This is The Burn today.

Dust Jacket and Book Design
by Robert Reynolds

Thomas K. Worcester - Editor

Binding by Lincoln & Allen
Lithography by The Irwin-Hodson Company